LUSH SALADS

Peter Pure

www.lushsalads.co.uk

First Edition published in Great Britain by Raw Food Party Ltd.

Photography: PETER PURE
Art Director: PETER PURE
Photo Retouching: MARGOT DOLEWSKA
Design & Typesetting: ATTILA CZINKE

Printed on acid-free paper.
Printed and bound in Turkey.

ISBN 978 0 9560058 0 9

1. Cookery (Natural foods) 2. Raw Foods

FREE SALAD VIDEO
Valued at £20

Peter Pure is creating a video to accompany this book. The video contains exclusive scenes of Peter in the kitchen providing you with some great salad tips, and showing techniques that are better demonstrated in videos.

Our initial offering of the video will be free for purchasers of this book.

To get your free salad video, go to:
www.lushsalads.co.uk/video

THE FUN REMEDY

Crazy food makes crazy people who make a crazy world.

This book of pure food will help empower you to create an amazing world.

ACKNOWLEDGEMENTS

Thank you to my father, who had me eat half a plate of salad every night. As a child I thought it would be cool to compile all the different raw salads. As an adult I thought it would be cool to create enough raw salads to fill a book.

Thank you to my team: Nuray, Lisa, Lavina, Kristina, Atidzhe, Margot, and Attila. You've all done your bit to help me create this book.

You're invited to our

Health & Performance Breakthrough Seminar

Would you like to transform your health and performance? To learn how, come to our seminar!

On the seminar you will learn:

- How to create massive amounts of personal energy
- How to boost your brain power, mental clarity and focus
- How to lose unwanted weight, the fun way
- How to increase your calmness
- The keys to beautiful skin
- How to protect yourself from osteoporosis
- How to solve health problems
- How to eliminate colds and flu's forever
- How to eliminate headaches forever
- How to eliminate the biggest source of toxins
- You will also learn how the foods you have eaten in the past continue to hinder you now, and what to do about it!

For more dates and details, go to
www.lushsalads.co.uk/breakthrough

Contents

Important Food Items & Kitchen Tools

To Begin

The Salads

Essential Foods & Condiments

These pages cover the key ingredients I've used in this book. They are store cupboard ingredients that will last for a long time. Have them on stand-by. All are really useful and help make your salads tasty.

The good news is that I've made your life easy! All of the items listed in these pages can be delivered to your door from our website www.lushsalads.co.uk. You can either get individual ingredients, or a package of the whole lot!

Agave

Agave is a sweet, but low glycemic syrup that comes from a cactus. It is useful to use in Asian dressings in place of normal sugar because it's a more natural product than sugar and more useful because it's already in liquid form.

Almond Butter

Almond butter, as opposed to peanut butter, because it turns out that peanuts actually have quite a lot of toxins on them that are bad for us. Almond butter is the healthy version of peanut butter.

Balsamic

To add taste, flavour and excitement to almost any salad or green leaf splash a bit of balsamic on it.

Like most things, there is the real deal, and then there are the cheap knock-offs. Cheap balsamic is quite horrible; whilst the real thing is delectable.

Balsamic is made from the left over pulp, skins and seeds from the wine making process. It is this pulp, which is then reduced and aged in a wooden barrel for 10 – 25 years. It comes out as a thick, sticky, delicious syrup.

Cheap balsamic is aged for maybe only one year, then mixed with huge quantities of red wine vinegar! And taste's yuck! In my book, if you want red wine vinegar, buy it separately.

The best thing about high quality balsamic is that whilst it costs more, because it's so concentrated you only need a few drops! Once you've tried a good bottle of balsamic, you won't ever go back! Go to www.lushsalads.co.uk and treat yourself to a lovely bottle of balsamic today!

Dijon Mustard

Originally, the mustard that was made in Dijon, France. The term designates a method for the making of mustard, in a particular fashion. It's an essential ingredient for many European dressings.

Himalayan Salt

Normal white table salt is demineralised and mixed with anti caking ingredients. Himalayan salt is a pure salt that comes from the Himalayan Mountains from an ancient seabed before the seas got polluted. Available from us at www.lushsalads.co.uk

Honey, runny

There are so many varieties of honey, and the taste really is dependent upon what flowers the bees have been feeding off.

I recommend three things: 1, get a runny honey -we'll be using it for certain salad dressings; runny honey is easy to mix. 2, get a honey that is fairly taste neutral. Whilst strongly flavoured honeys can be enjoyable, a taste neutral honey will be the most versatile. 3, Cheap honeys are loaded with refined sugar so bee keepers can take an indecent amount of honey from the bees. Not nice. Please get a decent honey made from 100% flower sap. Click on www.lushsalads.co.uk honey.

Linseed (Flax) Oil

Linseed oil tastes quite "buttery", but the main reason I use it so frequently in salad dressings is because it contains huge amounts of Omega 3 fats that are <u>essential</u> to human health and nutrition.

Omega 3 fats are crucial for brain function and are anti-inflammatory, amongst many other functions. But because they are so rare in our food, I recommend everyone use linseed oil in their salad dressings every day because it is an easy and tasty way to get Omega 3 fats in your diet.

Lastly, Linseed oil is very delicate and needs to be stored in the fridge; we have quality-controlled linseed oil at www.lushsalads.co.uk

Maple Syrup

The reduced sap from the Canadian Maple tree. It's a lovely rich sweet syrup that I use in marinades.

Mirin

Mirin is an essential naturally sweet condiment used in Japanese cuisine. It has it's own subtle flavour. I have used it in making authentic Japanese dressings.

Olives

There can be such a range of tastes and qualities with olives. I never used to like olives until I discovered that I just didn't like the cheap super saver olives! Having a Turkish wife, we have access to some of the nicest Turkish olives available anywhere. You too if you go to www.lushsalads.co.uk

Seaweeds

Seaweeds as a group are particularly high in minerals, which is important because most of us are demineralised. Hijiki, Wakame, Arame, Nori, Dulse, Mixed Seaweed Salad, it's all good and very easy to use, just soak in water for 30 minutes prior to use. I've used seaweeds a lot in the Japanese salads, and elsewhere to boost the nutrition. All these seaweeds you can get from us.

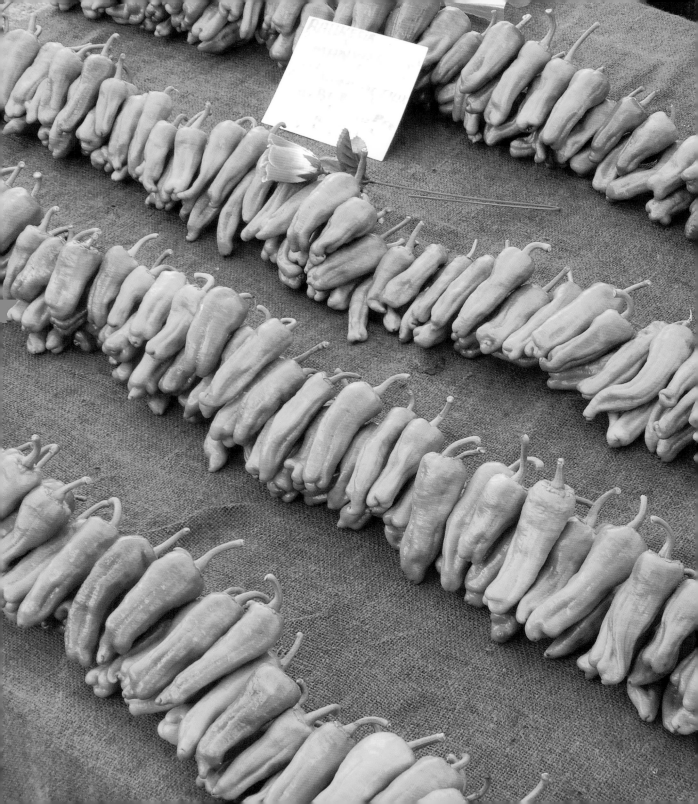

Tahini

Tahini is sesame seed paste, something that was being made over 3000 years ago in ancient Babylon. Sesame seeds are particularly rich in the mineral calcium. As a salad ingredient, I have used it to thicken up dressings particularly for Chinese dressings.

Tamari

Tamari is the healthier version of soy sauce with all the great taste. Since it is heavily fermented it appears that all the bad things about soy are not present in tamari. I have used it in almost every south East Asian salad as well as in marinades for transforming the taste of onions and mushrooms.

Vinegars

The word "vinegar" comes from old French "vin aigre", meaning "sour wine." Vinegar has been used since ancient times, even 3000 years ago, and is an important element in traditional cuisines around the world.

Vinegar is a liquid that comes from the fermentation of alcoholic beverages. Just as the quality of wines vary, so does the quality of wine vinegars. The best ones are matured in wood for up to two years and have a complex, mellow flavour.

The vinegars I have used in this book are: Rice vinegar for oriental salads, Red wine vinegar, White wine vinegar and Sherry vinegar for North European salads

White Miso

Miso is a traditional Japanese food produced by fermenting rice, barley or soybeans. It comes as a thick paste. In my experience, the darker in colour the miso, the darker and richer the taste. For the purposes of this book, I'm just sticking with white miso because the other miso's are just too heavy on the palate. I've used miso in the Japanese dressings, but it can also be a winner just mixed with a little orange juice as a dressing for green leaves.

HOW TO MAKE YOUR LIFE EASY

To make your life easy, all of the store cupboard items listed above can be delivered to you by clicking on www.lushsalads.co.uk

Notes on Food

The whole can be greater than the sum of the parts, but only if you use good parts!

Here follows some of my distinctions about foods that will help you create the tastiest recipes

Bell Peppers

Only red and yellow bell peppers are ripe. Green bell peppers are unripe and therefore demineralising. If you have a green bell pepper, leave it in a sunny window to ripen. It will go whatever colour it is supposed to.

Chillies

The smaller the chillies the hotter they are. The larger the chilli, the more mellow it tends to be. The seeds of chillies are particularly hot.

Limes

Limes are actually sold severely unripe, they should be yellow! If you get a green lime, put it in a sunny window until it ripens up. The only thing a green lime is good for is using a little bit of the peel to garnish.

Olives

We recommend you get really good quality olives because cheap olives taste bad. I actually didn't like olives for a long time until I realised I just didn't like the cheap and nasty ones. Have a look at our website www.lushsalads.co.uk for some of the tastiest olives we've ever met!

Onions

Red onions are generally mellower than yellow onions.

Quality

Food of any sort will only ever taste as good as the ingredients you are using. Fresher, fully ripe, in season ingredients not only taste better, they are better for you too. Cutting corners with cheap ingredients is also cutting corners with the taste and the health benefits.

Tomatoes

Smaller tomatoes are generally a lot sweeter than bigger tomatoes.

Kitchen Tools:
My Magnificent 7

Whilst salad can be as simple as tearing a green leaf and splashing some dressing on it. Here I'm listing the 7 tools that I find indispensable in creating salad magic.

1   MANDOLIN

The mandolin is perhaps the most useful tool of all to make salads. If I had to choose only one tool, a mandolin would be it. They are so useful, and I've used it for practically every recipe in this book.

Full time chefs have good knife skills, but with a mandolin you can cut quicker, finer, and more beautifully than even the most talented chef.

A good Japanese mandolin will come with a range of different blades for cutting many different types of cuts. It will also allow you to finely control the thickness of the cuts too.

You can get a good Japanese mandolin from our website www.lushsalads.co.uk

2 ZESTER

A zester is a super fine grater. The zester is really useful for lemon rind zest, lime rind zest, making ginger into a fine paste, garlic too.
You can get the same zester I use at www.lushsalads.co.uk

3 NOODLE MAKER

Ordinary noodles are 80% sugar, which switches off our immune systems and makes us fat. But guess what we're addicted to? The Shape!

The noodle maker tool allows you to make raw vegetable noodles out of various hard vegetables such as carrots, beetroot, parsnip, radish, pumpkin, butternut squash, sweet potato, and other roots and squashes. This is a great way to eat hard root vegetables raw, cut down on calories and increase your health. What about the taste? Simple; just add your favourite sauce.

The noodle maker comes with a few different blades so you can make noodles of varying thicknesses.

To get a noodle maker, go to www.lushsalads.co.uk

4 SHARP KNIFE

Obviously you need a knife! But is it sharp? When I run my chef training days I notice my students doing a whole lot of sawing because they are used to blunt old knifes that have been banging around in a drawer for years.

If you have ever seen the movie "Kill Bill", everything they say about Japanese steel is absolutely true. I've had expensive professional knives from other countries go blunt on me in a week. But my Japanese knives stay sharp for over a year without having to sharpen!

If you want to see the Japanese knife I'm delighted with, go to www.lushsalads.co.uk

5 SALAD SPINNER

A salad spinner is a great way to get the excess water off your salad leaves. It's an inexpensive tool that helps you make crisp salads. The only thing better than a salad spinner is a…

6 VEGGIE WASHER

If you're anything like me, you might have washed your food under a running tap for 3 seconds. Not very thoroughly! Imagine washing your clothes for 3 seconds!

A veggie washer is a kitchen counter washing machine for food. It can be programmed to wash your food for up to 10 minutes, then spin dry all your food afterward. Amazing.

A good veggie washer will also contain an ozone generator that is singlet oxygen. Bacteria, viruses, mould, pesticides, herbicides – they all get vaporised in the presence of singlet oxygen. Leaving you with a basket of squeaky clean food having been washed with nothing more than oxygen and water.

For veggie washers, see what's available at www.lushsalads.co.uk

7 AUTOMATIC SPROUTER

Young sprouted seeds and beans are on average 30 times more nutritious than the mature vegetable. There are simple sprouting tips with various recipes in this book. But if you want to get serious about having the best live nutrition grown cheaply and easily right at home, have a look at an automatic sprouter. See what's available at www.lushsalads.co.uk

DRESSINGS

Jazz up any salad with one of these tasty dressings

Simple Dressings

Keep it Simple Dressing

olive oil or linseed (flax) oil
lemon juice
Himalayan salt & freshly ground black pepper

Lemon & Parsley Dressing

2 tablespoons lemon juice
1 tablespoon olive oil
1 tablespoon linseed (flax) oil
1 teaspoon dried parsley
1 teaspoon lemon rind, finely grated on the zester
big pinch Himalayan salt

Blackberry Dressing

100g blackberries
¼ cup linseed (flax) oil
¼ teaspoon mixed spice (cinnamon, coriander seed, caraway, nutmeg, ginger, cloves)
pinch Himalayan salt

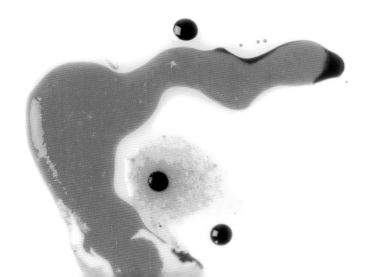

Classic Dressings

French Dressing

3 tablespoons olive oil or linseed (flax) oil
1 teaspoon white wine vinegar
1 teaspoon Dijon mustard
pinch Himalayan salt
pinch freshly ground black pepper

Pesto

80g basil leaves only, discard stems
60g pine nuts
1/3 cup olive oil
½ garlic clove
1/8 teaspoon Himalayan salt

Whiz up all the ingredients in a food processor until smooth. Adjust the salt and garlic to taste.

Pete's Caesar

2/3 cup cashews
1/3 cup white wine vinegar
½ cup olive oil
¼ cup water
1 garlic clove
1 teaspoon nutritional yeast
1 teaspoon Dijon mustard
1 teaspoon Himalayan salt
1 teaspoon black pepper
¼ teaspoon kelp powder

Put all the ingredients in a good blender and blend until completely smooth. This will make a reasonable quantity. This will keep in the fridge for a few days.

Creamy Dressings

Creamy Black Pepper Dressing

3 tablespoons cashew cream, (1 cup cashews blended until smooth with
1 cup water)
2 tablespoons linseed (flax) oil
2 tablespoons red wine vinegar
¼ teaspoon freshly ground black pepper
¼ teaspoon Himalayan salt

Put all the ingredients in a good blender and blend until completely smooth.
This dressing will keep in the fridge for a few days and will do for a few servings.

" I wanted a dressing that could take the place of
blue cheese in a recipe – this one
has been hitting the spot for all who have tried. "

Cashew Mayo

2/3 cup cashews
½ cup water
½ cup water
1 lemon, juiced
1 garlic clove
½ teaspoon Dijon mustard
¼ teaspoon Himalayan salt
freshly ground black pepper

In a blender, blend everything until smooth.

Oriental Dressings

Japanese Dressing

2 tablespoons mirin
2 tablespoons rice vinegar
1 tablespoon white miso (no other colour miso please! Only white!)

Thai Dressing

2 tablespoons tamari
1 tablespoon lime juice
1 teaspoon agave syrup
1/8 teaspoon garlic, zested
1/8 teaspoon red chilli, cut really small

Chinese Dressing

4 tablespoons tamari
2 tablespoons tahini
2 tablespoons honey (runny)
1 tablespoon ginger, zested
chilli flakes, big pinch

“ Why did the beetroot blush?
Because it saw the salad dressing! ”

So Many Leaves, Such Little Time

There is an infinite variety of green leaves, so many wild ones, and so many herbs. There is never a reason to have the same salad! In the following pages I'll cover some of the more common ones.

Mild Delicate Leaves

These are the leaves you can use all the time. They're so easy going, they're mostly looking for a supporting role to show case an exciting dressing or ingredient. These leaves are very delicate, so will need eating soon after applying the dressing.

Baby Spinach
Smaller, softer, and prettier than mature spinach. Spinach is amazingly nutritious. It's real "Popeye" food, and yet it's also very mild in taste. That's probably why it's used so much in so many cuisines.

Bulls Blood
Bulls blood is a member of the beetroot family. It can be used in mixed salads to create colour in your salads. It has a good shelf life compared to other coloured leaves.

Butterhead Lettuce
This is the classic flat leaf lettuce, it has a pleasant flavour and texture.

Lambs Lettuce
Also known as corn salad, Lambs lettuce has probably the most easy going and enjoyable flavour even in this section.

Oakleaf
Available in both red and green variations, it is a tender leaf with a mild flavour. It's a nice decorative addition to a salad.

Mild Crisp Leaves

These leaves are mild, but crisp and sturdy. In dressings, they will hold their form for much longer than the delicate leaves.

Romaine Lettuce
The French call it Romaine, the Greek call it Cos lettuce, named after the Greek island. It has a great flavour. It's crisp and light, yet sturdy. It's much more nutritious than Iceberg. It is also the only leaf to be used in a classic Caesar salad.

Iceberg Lettuce
In the UK, Iceberg has been the most ubiquitous leaf. It's crisp, durable, light yet sturdy, tastes of virtually nothing (so it won't upset anyone). It also has little nutritional content.

Little Gem Lettuce
Comes in both green and red varieties. In some ways they are like a miniature romaine lettuce. Mild and crispy, they can be great just quartered and served as finger food with a good dressing.

Robust Leaves

Kale
Kale is densley nutritious, and robust. It comes in a variety of colours: green, purple and black. Kale is best wilted manually with your hands in salt, lemon and olive oil.

Baby Bok Choy
Also known as Pak Choi, Bok Choy is the English name for Chinese Cabbage, which is called "bai cai" in Mandarin. Bok choy is tougher than a lettuce, but more tender and milder than normal cabbages. It is strong and resilient. Mature bok choy often is not much tougher than the baby one, so you can use either.

Sprouts

Sprouted seeds and small beans of all kinds are especially high in nutritional value, much more than the mature plant. For your health, consume them at every opportunity.

Any mature vegetable, you can get the seeds and make baby sprouts out of them: adzuki bean, alfalfa, broccoli, fenugreek, garlic, mung bean, onion, peas, radish, sunflower sprouts – this list goes on forever! If you really want to get serious about your health, get an automatic sprouter to make your sprouting life easier. See our automatic sprouters at www.lushsalads.co.uk

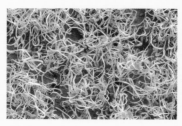

Alfalfa
Alfalfa is particularly mild, and very easy to sprout. You can put it in almost any salad and it won't affect the taste too much. Alfalfa sprouts can even be bought from some supermarkets these days.

Bitter Leaves

Bitter is a taste that signifies nutrition being present. They are good mixed with a variety of stronger flavours to help mask their bitterness.

Chicory
Also known as endive or Belgian endive. Chicory is mildly bitter and quite robust.

Dandelion
Strong, nutritious, and bitter is how I describe dandelion. It grows wild almost everywhere. I think it's best consumed with other salad greens as it can be quite strong on its own.

Radicchio
Developed from chicory. It has a beautiful colour that contrasts nicely with green leaves. It is mildly bitter.

Cabbages

Hugely robust and crunchy, leaving dressings on cabbages usually improves the taste. Leaving a dressing on a cabbage for 3 – 30 hours softens them up and makes them more digestible whilst retaining their crunchiness. Technically speaking, bok choy would also be in this group.

Chinese Leaf
Chinese leaf is perhaps the mildest out of all the cabbages. Crunchy, yet light in flavour.

Red & White Cabbages

Colourful and crunchy, these are the common cabbage. They are especially good when left sitting for a day in a simple Himalayan salt, olive oil and lemon juice dressing.

Savoy Cabbage

Stronger tasting than other cabbages. This cabbage is best shredded fine and mixed with crunchy vegetables and other varieties of cabbages.

Fragrant Leaves

In the West we tend to consider herbs as a flavouring ingredient. However, in many countries, they are used as the main salad leaf.

Basil

Basil is a classic herb used in Mediterranean cuisine. Making a whole salad out of basil is very tasty mixed with other Mediterranean ingredients. There is also Greek basil which has really small leaves, and Thai basil which is harder than the Mediterranean basil.

Coriander

In USA they call it cilantro. Some people love it, some people hate it. For sure you can make a whole salad out of coriander, it has a great flavour and soft leaves. It is also a good detoxifier of mercury.

Flat Leaf Parsley

Flat leaf parsley (as opposed to curly parsley) has a vibrant flavour, and is rich in calcium. Can be mixed with mint as the basis for an eastern salad.

Sorrel
Grows great in the wild, sorrel has an amazing lemon like flavour to it. It's good for the kidneys and rich in nutrients.

Peppery Leaves

Having an element of spiciness, peppery leaves can be a delicious back bone to many salads. They can also be mixed in with mild leaves. These leaves are also quite delicate, so will need to be eaten soon after dressing.

Chard
Also known as swiss chard and silverbeet. It is only very mildly peppery. It is from the same family as beetroot. In this picture we have red chard, but it also comes in green.

Mizuna
Mizuna grows in temperate climates as a weed. Originally from Japan, it has a great peppery flavour. Can be used instead of rocket. It is moderately robust in salads.

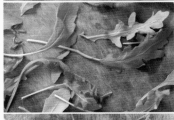

Rocket
Known in the USA as Arugula. Rocket is one of the few wild plants you can find in a supermarket, although it is increasingly being farmed. It has a superb flavour that livens up salads.

Watercress
Grows in the wild next to streams. Watercress has a distinctive flavour. Nice mixed with just a few other simple salad ingredients or use as a garnish.

Dips

If **you** Bring a Crudi
Dip

te, I'll **Bring a**

Cashew Hummus

Serves 2

1 cup cashews
½ cup water
½ courgette (zucchini), green skin peeled off, use white segment only
1 tablespoon tahini
1 small lemon, juiced
1/3 teaspoon cumin
¼ teaspoon Himalayan salt

Peel off and discard the green skin from the courgette. Put all ingredients into a powerful blender and blend until smooth. Important – put the tahini in the blender last, otherwise the mixture might not turn over properly.

" In England, we call it Houmous, the word comes from arabic: Hummus which means chickpeas. Some people use sprouted chickpeas, but I don't like the taste too much, find that they are too full of sugar, and like most people, find any quantity of sprouted chickpeas hard to digest. As a recipe Hummus is one of the oldest known prepared foods, with a long history in the Middle East which stretches back to antiquity. "

Sunflower Pate

1 cup sunflower seeds, soaked overnight, washed and drained.
¼ cup linseed (flax) oil or olive oil
¼ cup water
1 or 2 lemons, juiced
1 teaspoon Himalayan salt
1 clove of garlic

OPTIONAL INGREDIENTS TO CHOOSE FROM
TO ADD MORE TASTE AND FLAVOUR
Herbs chopped fine: parsley, dill, coriander (cilantro)
Vegetables: finely chopped celery, bell pepper, onion, olives
Spices: chilli pepper, curry powder, cumin

1   Put all the pate ingredients in a food processor and process until smooth. If it is too thick and not turning over properly, add a little more water. We're aiming for a thick hummus like consistency.

2   When the pate is relatively smooth, turn the mixture out into a bowl and mix in any additional ingredients by hand.

This pate is so versatile; it can be near enough anything you want it to be! On it's own it's delicious. But mixing in other ingredients gives you lots of variety:

- Add cumin and you have a hummus.
- Jazz up the basic hummus by adding sun dried tomatoes or olives.
- Add curry powder, chilli and coriander (cilantro) and you have a curry pate.
- Add kelp powder, dill, celery and onion and you have a seafood taste.
- Switch the lemon juice for lime juice, add lemongrass, tamari (instead of salt) and ginger and we're off to Thailand!

Almond Satay Sauce

Serves 1 - 2

170g jar raw almond butter
1 - 2 garlic cloves, zested
thumbsize ginger, zested
1 – 3 tablespoons tamari, to taste
1 – 2 teaspoons honey or agave syrup
cayenne pepper or fresh red chilli, chopped small, to taste

Either in a food processor, or with a fork, mix up all the ingredients until smooth. You will need to add a small amount of water to adjust the consistency, it should be thick, but somewhat runny.

The recipe should be a blend of spicy-ness, salty-ness (which comes from the tamari) and just a tiny bit sweet. Adjust the variables to your liking.

" As a child I would eat peanut butter everyday, but later in life I learnt that peanuts contain lots of mycotoxins, so I switched to almond butter. This has to be one of the tastiest dips for raw vegetable and raw broccoli in particular. When I demonstrate this sauce on classes, I try and hide the mixing bowl from my kitchen team so I can get to eat some later. Trouble is my team are so ingenious that they usually find it and eat it all by the time it's my break! "

Guacamole

2 avocados, peeled and stones removed
½ lime, juiced
pinch Himalayan salt

Optional ingredients:
1 teaspoon coriander (cilantro), chopped
1 teaspoon tomato, diced
1 teaspoon onion, diced
jalapeno peppers to taste

Put the avocados, salt and lime juice in a food processor. Mix until smooth. Turn out of the mixture out of the food processor into a bowl and by hand mix in the coriander, tomato and onion.

" Of Aztec origin, Guacamole was originally made by mashing avocado with a type of pestle and mortar, adding tomatoes and salt. The name guacamole comes from the Nahuatl language of the Aztecs āhuacamolli, āhuacatl (avocado) + molli (sauce). "

North
Europ

ern
e

Green Beans & Peach Salad

Serves 1

FOR THE SALAD

100g green beans cut 4cm long
50g whole cashews
1 peach, cut into slices
10g fresh mint leaves
10g fresh basil leaves

FOR THE DRESSING

1 tablespoon linseed (flax) seed oil, drizzle on top of salad
1 tablespoon balsamic vinegar, drizzle on top of salad

" Whilst writing this book I discovered that peaches originally come from Asia, and both peaches and nectarines grow on the same tree! – only some grow fuzzy and some don't. "

Norwegian Berry

Serves 1

FOR THE SALAD

50g baby spinach
1 conference pear, sliced wafer thin lengthwise on the mandolin
1 small handful walnuts
1 small handful blueberries

FOR THE DRESSING

3 tablespoon creamed cashews (1 cup cashews blended with 1 cup water until smooth)
2 tablespoons linseed (flax) oil
2 tablespoons red wine vinegar
¼ teaspoon freshly ground black pepper
¼ teaspoon Himalayan salt

"
We were conducting a retreat in Norway, and around us in the mountains was a huge variety of delightful berries, most of which I have never seen or heard of. So every day of the retreat I figured out a few new ways to take advantage of the wild berries, including putting them in salads.
"

Broad Bean & Dill

Serves 1

FOR THE SALAD

200g broad beans, fresh
80g kalamata olives
40g pine nuts
1 red bell pepper, diced fine
4 tablespoons dill, chopped small

FOR THE DRESSING

1 lemon, juiced
2 tablespoons olive oil
pinch Himalayan salt
freshly ground black pepper

Broad beans come in a long pod, inside the pod is the bean. The beans
themselves have a skin that is edible, but the beans will be even more tasty
and succulent if you peel the skin off.

Dressed Little Gem Lettuces

2 little gem lettuces, quartered

FOR PETE'S CAESAR DRESSING

2/3 cup cashews
1/3 cup white wine vinegar
½ cup olive oil
¼ cup water
1 garlic clove
1 teaspoon nutritional yeast
1 teaspoon Dijon mustard
1 teaspoon Himalayan salt
1 teaspoon black pepper
¼ teaspoon kelp powder

Put all the dressing ingredients in a blender and blend until smooth.
This will make a reasonable quantity. It will last in the fridge for a while.

> "This is real finger food, and quartered little gem lettuces are about the same size as chocolate buns. So the next time the girls are around for a social, instead of a plate of cakes, present them these dressed little gems."

Herb Garden Salad

Serves 1 - 2

FOR THE SALAD

75g coriander (cilantro) or parsley, chopped
90g soaked sun dried tomatoes, cut into strips
135g mixed bean sprouts, mung, green lentil, brown lentil, adzuki
75g black olives

FOR THE DRESSING

1 tablespoon lemon juice
1 tablespoon olive oil
pinch freshly ground black pepper
pinch Himalayan salt

MIXED BEAN SPROUTS
You can buy packs of mixed sprouts these days from a supermarket. Or to grow them yourself, soak the raw lentils and beans in water overnight, then drain and leave them in a colander the next morning. Rinse water through the lentils and beans in the colander 2 times per day, and after a few days they will be ready. Alternatively, get yourself an automatic sprouter such as the Easy Green, which does all the work for you and produces a superior result. Automatic sprouters are available from www.lushsalads.co.uk

"
Whilst plants such as parsley and coriander are often
considered as flavouring herbs,
in many countries they are used as the salads themselves.
"

Watercress Wakame Salad

Serves 1

FOR THE SALAD

150g watercrees
50g alfalfa
20g wakame, soaked ½ hour in water
1 pear, sliced thin on the mandolin
½ -1 avocado, sliced

FOR THE DRESSING

2 tablespoons lemon juice
2 tablespoons linseed (flax) seed oil
½ teaspoon horseradish sauce

I'm always on the lookout for increasing the nutritional levels of my food. This salad is not only highly nutritious; in our taste scores our testers marked it as a 10.

Rocket (Arugula) & Peach Salad

Serves 1 - 2

FOR THE SALAD

100g rocket
2 red radishes
1 peach, sliced

FOR THE FRENCH DRESSING

3 tablespoons linseed (flax) oil or olive oil
1 teaspoon white wine vinegar
1 teaspoon Dijon mustard
pinch Himalayan salt
pinch freshly ground black pepper

Toss the rocket in the French dressing, garnish with the peach and radish.

Rocket is one of the few wild plants you can get from a
supermarket, although it is now sometimes cultivated.
It has been grown in the Mediterranean area since
Roman times, and was considered an aphrodisiac.

Pea, Mint & Olive Salad

Serves 1

FOR THE SALAD

300g peas
120g sprouted quinoa
60g black olives
60g cashews, soaked in water for 2 hours, water discarded
40g baby spinach
20 mint leaves

FOR THE DRESSING

2 tablespoons lemon juice
1 tablespoon olive oil
pinch Himalayan salt

 Peas and mint are such a classic English combination. Why not make a meal of it?!

Rocket, Date & Red Onion Salad

Serves 1

FOR THE SALAD

60g rocket, or mizuna
1 stick of celery, chopped
½ small red onion, finely sliced
4 medjool dates, chopped finely

FOR THE FRENCH DRESSING

3 tablespoons olive oil or linseed oil
1 teaspoon white wine vinegar
1 teaspoon Dijon mustard
Himalayan salt & black pepper

My parents would make a simple salad with grated carrot,
celery, apple, then add onion and chopped date.
The combination of onion and date is a real winner.

Sprouted Beans in Spicy Tomato Sauce

Serves 2

FOR THE SALAD

200g mixed bean sprouts: green lentil, brown lentil, adzuki beans, mung beans, and chickpeas
1 red bell pepper, diced small
3 spring onion (scallion), sliced fine
¼ teaspoon chilli flakes

FOR THE BELLPEPPER & TOMATO SAUCE

1 red bell pepper
100g sun dried tomatoes, soaked in water overnight
50g fresh tomatoes
¼ cup olive oil
1 teaspoon curry powder
1/3 teaspoon Himalayan salt

1 You can buy packs of mixed sprouts these days from a supermarket. Or to grow them yourself, soak the raw lentils and beans in water overnight, then drain and leave them in a colander the next morning. Rinse water through the lentils and beans in the colander 2 times per day, and after a few days they will be ready. Alternatively, get yourself an automatic sprouter such as the Easy Green, which does all the work for you and produces a superior result. Automatic sprouters are available from www.lushsalads.co.uk

2 For the tomato-pepper sauce, put the fresh tomatoes in a blender first, then the bell pepper, finally everything else. It is important that you do it in this order otherwise the mixture won't blend. Blend until smooth.

Watercress & Avocado Salad

Serves 1

FOR THE SALAD

40g watercress, tear apart with your fingers
½ avocado, chunky cubes
1-2 tomatoes, diced
½ small red onion, sliced

FOR THE DRESSING

1 tablespoon olive oil
pinch Himalayan salt

"
Watercress is a fast-growing plant that grows in water. It is
native to Europe and central Asia, and is one of the
oldest known leaf vegetables
consumed by human beings. It has a peppery, tangy flavour.
"

Blackberry & Caramelised Onion Salad

Serves 2

FOR THE SALAD

100g mixed leaves
1 small red onion, marinated
almonds, or other nut to garnish

FOR THE ONION MARINADE

2 tablespoons maple syrup
2 tablespoons olive oil
2 tablespoons tamari

FOR THE BLACKBERRY DRESSING

100g blackberries
¼ cup linseed (flax) oil
¼ teaspoon mixed spice (cinnamon, coriander seed, caraway, nutmeg, ginger, cloves)
pinch Himalayan salt

1 Marinate the sliced onion for 2 hours.

2 Put all the blackberry dressing ingredients into a blender, and blend until smooth.

Waldorf Salad

Serves 1 - 2

FOR THE SALAD

2 apples, sliced into thin wedges
8 sticks of celery, sliced fine
1 cup walnuts

FOR THE CASHEW MAYO

2/3 cup cashews
½ cup water
1 lemon, juiced
1 garlic clove
1 teaspoon Dijon mustard
¼ teaspoon Himalayan salt
freshly ground black pepper

Blend all the cashew mayo ingredients in a blender until smooth.
Mix mayo with apple, celery and walnuts, coating thoroughly.

" What a classic! First created around 1893 at the Waldorf Hotel in New York City. Oscar Tschirky, was the maître d'hôtel at the Waldorf, and in 1896 Waldorf Salad appeared in "The Cook Book by 'Oscar of the Waldorf'". It is traditionally served on lettuce. Dried fruit is often added - usually chopped dates or raisins. "

Lambs Lettuce & Beetroot

Serves 1

FOR THE SALAD

60g lambs lettuce (corn salad)
1 small beetroot, sliced wafer thin on the mandolin, marinated
1 spring onion, sliced thin
1 tablespoon dill to garnish

FOR THE FRENCH DRESSING

3 tablespoons olive oil
1 teaspoon white wine vinegar
1 teaspoon Dijon mustard
pinch Himalayan salt & freshly ground black pepper

FOR THE BEETROOT MARINADE

½ lemon, juiced
2 tablespoons olive oil
generous pinch Himalayan salt

Marinate the beetroot for an hour to soften it slightly.

The real trick to making hard vegetables like beetroot edible
raw is to cut them small enough. You can actually get
away with anything if you cut it small enough and mix
it with other items. Here, slicing the beetroot as fine as
you possibly can is the key. This is where the thickness
adjustment on a good mandolin comes in handy.

Kale Avocado

Serves 2 - 3

FOR THE SALAD

200g kale, chopped
6 tomatoes, cut into quarters
1 ripe avocado
1 garlic clove, zested
1 lemon, juiced
pinch cayenne pepper
pinch Himalayan salt

Place all the ingredients in the bowl and squeeze everything together with your hands until everything is well mixed and the avocado becomes creamy and mayonnaise like!

The first person to make this recipe for me was the raw food chef Chad Sarno. In my opinion it is a simple and delicious classic.

Cricket & Wimbledon Salad

Serves 1

FOR THE SALAD

½ cucumber, sliced fine on the mandolin
1 peach, cut into fine cubes
2 tablespoons dill, finely chopped

FOR THE DRESSING

1 tablespoon orange juice
1 tablespoon linseed (flax) oil
1 teaspoon white wine vinegar
pinch Himalayan salt

66

Great traditional sports in England are cricket and tennis.
If I was commissioned to come up with a salad by the
Wimbledon committee and Lords, this would be
my perfect English salad that would proudly sit
next to the Pimms, cucumber sandwiches and
strawberries normally enjoyed at these events. Bravo Chaps!

99

Alfalfa, Asparagus & Pea Salad

Serves 1

FOR THE SALAD

150g raw baby peas, otherwise frozen peas
90g asparagus, sliced fine
60g alfalfa sprouts
5 tablespoons chives, chopped fine

FOR THE DRESSING

3 tablespoons linseed (flax) oil
1 small lemon, juiced
1 teaspoon horseradish sauce
pinch Himalayan salt

Apple, Fennel & Cucumber

Serves 1

FOR THE SALAD

1 cucumber, sliced thin on the mandolin
1 small fennel, sliced thin on the mandolin
1 apple, sliced into matchsticks on the mandolin
7 mint leaves, cut into thin strips

FOR THE DRESSING

2 tablespoons of lime juice
2 tablespoons of linseed (flax) oil
generous pinch of freshly ground black pepper

I make a variation of this salad in a juice, it is highly refreshing,
light and enjoyable. It could
even be served as a palate freshener between courses.

Pear & Watercress Salad

Serves 1 - 2

FOR THE SALAD

35g romaine lettuce
35g watercress
1 small conference pear, cut into fine noodles on the mandolin
5 small radishes, sliced
hazelnuts, to garnish

FOR THE DRESSING

1 tablespoon olive oil
freshly ground black pepper

Radicchio, Parsley & Creamy Black Pepper Dressing

Serves 2

FOR THE SALAD

1 cucumber, sliced fine on the mandolin
1 head of radicchio lettuce, torn into small pieces
250g cherry tomatoes, halved
parsley to garnish

FOR THE DRESSING

3 tablespoons creamed cashews – (1 cup of cashews blended with 1 cup of water until smooth)
2 tablespoons linseed (flax) oil
2 tablespoons red wine vinegar
¼ teaspoon black pepper
¼ teaspoon Himalayan salt

In this salad the cucumber and tomatoes balance out the bitterness of the radicchio.

Wild Dandelion & Maple Marinated Pear

Serves 2

FOR THE SALAD

Bunch of fresh, wild dandelion greens. Otherwise use a mixture of rocket, watercress, mizuna
1 pear, cut into ½ cm thick slices
pine nuts to garnish

FOR THE PEAR MARINADE

¼ cup maple syrup
½ teaspoon Himalayan salt

FOR THE DRESSING

1 tablespoon olive oil
1 teaspoon red wine vinegar
big pinch freshly ground black pepper
pinch Himalayan salt

Marinade the pear for at least 1 hour or more.

" This is a raw equivalent to roasted pear. The sweetness of the pear balances out the bitterness of the dandelion. "

Sprouted Quinoa & Plum Salad

Serves 1

FOR THE SALAD

    30g lambs lettuce (corn salad)
    2 plums, diced
    2 tablespoons sprouted quinoa

FOR THE DRESSING

    1 tablespoon linseed (flax) oil
    drizzle balsamic vinegar
    pinch Himalayan salt

TO SPROUT THE QUINOA
Soak the quinoa in water overnight. It will start to sprout very quickly, strain the water off the next day, the sprouts will be ready.

" Quinoa contains a balance of essential amino acids and is gluten free. "

Wild Brittania

Serves 1

FOR THE SALAD

    60g lambs lettuce (corn salad)
    5 rose petals
    blackberries, handful
    walnuts, handful

CHOOSE A DRESSING:

DRESSING 1

    1 tablespoon lemon juice
    1 tablespoon linseed (flax) oil
    pinch Himalayan salt

DRESSING 2

    1 tablespoon sherry vinegar
    1 tablespoon linseed (flax) oil
    pinch Himalayan salt

“ Wild food is a lot more nutritious than shop bought food,
and it's also free – so can fit anyone's budget! Trouble is, most
of what is wild generally doesn't taste very good.
Here I had a look around the garden and used what I could. ”

Sunflower "Spaghetti"

Serves 1 - 2

FOR THE SALAD

150g long sunflower sprouts
120g kalamata olives
1 small garlic clove, zested
pine nuts to garnish

FOR THE DRESSING

1 tablespoon linseed (flax) oil
balsamic, drizzle on top

" We grow our own sunflower sprouts from the black sunflower seeds with hulls on them in our automatic sprouter. After about 7 days they grow really long. This is one of my favourite salads because it's so nutritious and it reminds me of eating spaghetti. "

Pear & Pecan Salad with Cashew – Black Pepper Dressing

Serves 1 - 2

FOR THE SALAD

200g mixed lettuce, torn
1 pear, sliced fine on mandolin
pecans, to garnish

FOR THE DRESSING

3 tablespoons cashew cream, (1 cup cashews blended until smooth with
1 cup water)
2 tablespoons linseed (flax) oil
2 tablespoons red wine vinegar
¼ teaspoon freshly ground black pepper
¼ teaspoon Himalayan salt

This dressing will keep in the fridge for a few days and will do for a few servings.

Mizuna, Avocado & Pink Grapefruit

Serves 1 - 2

FOR THE SALAD

90g mizuna or rocket (arugula)
1 pink grapefruit, cut into segments
1 avocado, cut in slices

FOR THE DRESSING

3 tablespoons linseed (flax) oil
3 tablespoons lime juice
1 teaspoon coriander seed, cracked
freshly ground black pepper
pinch Himalayan salt

TO CRACK CORIANDER SEEDS
You can crack coriander seed either with a pestle
and mortar or with the back of a tablespoon on a
hard surface.

TO CUT THE GRAPEFRUIT SEGMENTS
1 With a sharp knife, cut the top and the bottom
off the grapefruit so that the flesh is exposed.

2 Slice off the remainder of the skin, removing all
the rind and a little of the inner skin.

3 With the knife, cut either side of the skin that
divides the segments.

Lemon, Coconut & Mizuna

Serves 1

FOR THE SALAD

25g mizuna or rocket (arugula)
jelly from 1 green coconut cut into strips
1 baby aubergine (eggplant), sliced and marinated for 3 hours

FOR THE DRESSING

1 tablespoon lime juice
1 tablespoon linseed (flax) oil
1/3 teaspoon lemon rind, zested
big pinch freshly ground black pepper

FOR THE AUBERGINE MARINADE

¼ cup olive oil
¼ cup tamari

" Coconut jelly from young green coconuts can be a real delight to work with. It can double up as noodles, or it can be used in the place of seafood, which is what I did here. "

Rocket, Fennel & Pink Grape Fruit

Serves 1

FOR THE SALAD

    50g rocket
    ½ fennel shaved on the mandolin
    ½ pink grapefruit, cut into segments
    walnuts, handful to garnish

FOR THE FRENCH DRESSING

    3 tablespoons linseed (flax) oil or olive oil
    1 teaspoon white wine vinegar
    1 teaspoon Dijon mustard
    pinch Himalayan salt
    pinch freshly ground black pepper

TO CUT THE GRAPEFRUIT SEGMENTS
1 With a sharp knife, cut the top and the bottom off the grapefruit so that the flesh is exposed.

2 Slice off the remainder of the skin, removing all the rind and a little of the inner skin.

3 With the knife, cut either side of the skin that divides the segments.

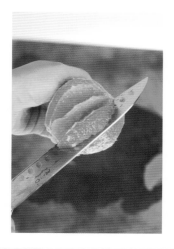

Fig, Cantaloupe & Wakame Salad

Serves 1

FOR THE SALAD

    ¼ cantaloupe melon, cubed
    2 figs, quartered
    10g dry wakame seaweed, soaked in fresh water for 30 minutes

Take the wakame out of the water and discard the water. Mix everything else together.

 This salad would normally be made with ham instead of wakame, but I've switched to wakame, which is by far more nutritious and it tastes fabulous.

Fennel & Asparagus Salad

Serves 1

FOR THE SALAD

 1 fennel, shaved into fine slices on the mandolin
 10 asparagus, shaved on the mandolin or sliced very thinly with a knife

FOR THE DRESSING

 1 tablespoon lemon
 1 tablespoon honey
 1 tablespoon olive oil
 1 tablespoon white wine vinegar
 pinch Himalayan salt and black pepper

 This salad can make a great accompaniment to other dishes.

Mooli & Beetroot Spiral Salad

Serves 1 as a side salad

FOR THE SALAD

75g mooli (daikon), spiralised on the noodle maker
75g beetroot, spiralised on the noodle maker
parsley leaves
handful black olives

FOR THE DRESSING

1 tablespoon linseed (flax) oil
1 tablespoon lemon juice
pinch Himalayan salt

Mooli is a large radish. You could also use ordinary red radishes for this.

Using a spiraliser is a great way to consume and present hard
root vegetables and winter squashes.
This salad would be good with food from the sea.

Kale Dill Salad

Serves 1

FOR THE SALAD

1 red bell pepper, diced
1 cob of sweet corn, corn cut off
60g kale, chopped
40g onion, sliced fine
20g dill, chopped
2 tomatoes, diced
1 avocado, diced
2 - 4 tablespoons of tomato chilli paste

FOR THE TOMATO CHILLI PASTE

200g sun dried tomato, soak them in the water for a few hours if hard
½ cup olive oil
1 fresh tomato
1 tablespoon ginger, zested
2 garlic cloves
1/8 teaspoon turmeric
¼ teaspoon fresh chilli pepper

Put all the tomato chilli paste ingredients into a good blender or food processor and whiz it up. It will turn into a paste. This recipe will produce more than you need for 1 salad but it keeps well in the fridge. So put the surplus paste in a glass jar and it will be a very delicious spread or sauce ready for you!

How to cut the corn off the cob

Beans, Sprouts & Tamarind Tomatoes

Serves 1 - 2

FOR THE SALAD

200g broad beans, shelled and peeled
100g tomatoes, chopped
50g mixed bean sprouts: aduzki, mung, green lentil, brown lentil, chickpea
2 tablespoons parsley, chopped fine
1 spring onion (scallion), sliced
1 tablespoon tamarind paste
1 garlic clove, zested

TO MAKE TAMARIND SAUCE

Whilst you can buy whole tamarind, peeling it and getting the pips out of it is a real pain. We buy tamarind in block form that has already been peeled and pipped. Break some tamarind off the block and soak it in water for a few hours, then blend it with a little water into a thick paste.

MIXED BEAN SPROUTS

You can buy packs of mixed sprouts these days from a supermarket. Or to grow them yourself, soak the raw lentils and beans in water overnight, then drain and leave them in a colander the next morning. Rinse water through the lentils and beans in the colander 2 times per day, and after a few days they will be ready. Alternatively, get yourself an automatic sprouter such as the Easy Green, which does all the work for you and produces a superior result. Automatic sprouters are available from www.lushsalads.co.uk

BROADBEANS

Broad beans come in a long pod, inside the pod is the bean. The beans themselves have a skin that is edible, but the beans will be even more tasty and succulent if you peel the skin off.

Lentil Sprout & Parsley Salad

Serves 1 - 2

FOR THE SALAD

200g green lentil sprouts
80g black olives
60g chopped parsley
2 small tomatoes, diced
2 small red onions, sliced fine

FOR THE DRESSING

1 lemon, juiced
dash olive oil
pinch Himalayan salt

TO MAKE THE LENTIL SPROUTS
Soak the green lentils overnight. Next day, drain the water, rinse the lentils and leave them in a colander. After that, rinse the lentils in the colander with fresh water twice a day, every day. They will be ready in 3-5 days.

Winter Root Salad

Serves 1 - 2

FOR THE SALAD

200g sugar snap beans, sliced fine
2 carrots, cut into matchsticks on the mandolin
2 beetroots, cut into matchsticks on the mandolin
50g hazelnuts
baby sprouts to garnish (optional), I've used cress and red radish sprouts

FOR THE FRENCH DRESSING

6 tablespoons linseed (flax) oil or olive oil
1 tablespoon white wine vinegar
1 tablespoon Dijon mustard
pinch Himalayan salt and freshly ground black pepper

This is a hearty salad for the winter. Raw food and salads
can actually be warmed up in several ways;
1, Flash heat it in an oven for a minute or two.
2, Place in a warm bowl to serve.
3, Blanch the whole salad in hot
water for 1 minute, then drain the water before serving.

Coleslaw with Cashew Mayo

Serves 2 - 3

FOR THE SALAD

200g grated white cabbage
200g grated carrots

FOR THE CASHEW MAYO

1½ cups cashews
1 cup water
3 lemons, juiced
4 medium garlic cloves
¼ teaspoon Himalayan salt

Blend the mayo ingredients in a blender until smooth. If needed add more lemon juice or water. You can actually get away with putting tons of raw garlic in this recipe because the cashews totally mellow out the garlic kick.

The name Cole slaw, arose in the 18th century as a partial translation from the Dutch term "koolsla", a shortening of "koolsalade", which means cabbage salad. It was commonly called cold slaw in Britain until the 1860s when "cole" (meaning cabbage) was revived.

Cabbage Slaw

Serves 1

FOR THE SALAD

    100g red cabbage, sliced fine on the mandolin
    50g savoy cabbage, sliced fine on the mandolin
    ½ red pepper, sliced into fine strips
    1 small red onion, sliced fine

FOR THE DRESSING

    1 lemon, juiced
    2 – 3 tablespoons olive oil
    ½ teaspoon Himalayan salt

Shoots & Roots

Serves 1 or 2

FOR THE SALAD

¼ celeriac, grated on mandolin
2 sticks of celery
100g mixed sprouts; mung bean, green and brown lentil, adzuki bean and chickpea
1 large carrot, grated
1 small fennel, sliced fine on the mandolin
¼ red onion, finely diced
¼ cup raisins
3 tablespoons of cashew mayo

FOR THE CASHEW MAYO

2/3 cup cashews
½ cup water
1 lemon, juiced
½ cup water
1 garlic clove
½ teaspoon Dijon mustard
¼ teaspoon Himalayan salt
freshly ground black pepper

Put all the cashew mayo ingredients in a good blender and blend until smooth.

> " To garnish I have used tiny sprouts. In the culinary world, little sprouts are called micro greens. "

Radish Canapé

Serves 1

10 red radishes
20g black olive flesh
20g green olive flesh
15g capers
pinch Himalayan salt

1 Cut the tops off the radishes, cut a small piece off the bottom to create a flat base for it to stand. Next scoop out a little of the inside of the radish to put the topping in.

2 Trim the flesh off the olives and mince fine. Mix the olive flesh, capers and salt and then fill the radishes.

Mediter

pranean

Heirloom Tomato

Serves 1

FOR THE SALAD

    heirloom tomatoes
    1 – 2 teaspoons olive oil
    balsamic
    pinch Himalayan salt

" This is so simple, and yet so delightful when different looking
tomatoes are used. Heirloom tomatoes are also known as
Heritage tomatoes, they are original cultivars, not hybridised,
and are uniquely beautiful. You could also add some
other classic Italian ingredients such as pine nuts and basil. "

Aubergine (Eggplant) & Tomato

Serves 1

FOR THE SALAD

3 baby aubergines, sliced very finely
¼ cup olive oil
¼ cup tamari
chives, chopped fine to garnish

FOR THE TOMATO CHILLI PASTE

200g sun dried tomato, soak them in water for a few hours if hard
½ cup olive oil
1 fresh tomato
1 tablespoon ginger, zested
2 garlic cloves
1/8 teaspoon turmeric
¼ teaspoon fresh chilli pepper

1 Put all the tomato chilli paste ingredients in a good blender or food processor and whiz it up. It will turn into a paste. If you want to make the sauce lighter or runnier, just add some more fresh tomatoes. This recipe will produce more than you need for 1 salad but it keeps well in the fridge. So put the surplus paste in a glass jar and it will be a very delicious spread or sauce ready for you!

2 After slicing the aubergines, marinate them in the olive oil and tamari for at least 2 hours.

3 When marinated, put the aubergine on a plate and add the Tomato Chilli Sauce on them and sprinkle chopped chives to garnish.

Spanish Salad

Serves 1 - 2

FOR THE SALAD

100g tomatoes, diced
50g watercress
50g green jumbo olives
30g black olives
2 spring onion (scallion), sliced
1 tablespoon capers

FOR THE DRESSING

1 tablespoon olive oil
¼ teaspoon garlic, zested
1/8 teaspoon paprika
1/8 teaspoon cumin

" Adding spices to salads is a great way to add
flavour, spices are also very good for you. "

Rocket & Beans with Pesto

Serves 1

FOR THE SALAD

70g mange tout, cut into diamonds
70g sugar snaps, cut into diamonds
20g rocket (arugula)
55g sun dried tomato, soak them in the water for a few hours if hard
handful pine nuts
1 tablespoon capers
2 tablespoons pesto

FOR THE PESTO

80g basil leaves, discard stems
60g pine nuts
1/3 cup olive oil
1 teaspoon nutritional yeast flakes (optional)
½ garlic clove
1/8 teaspoon Himalayan salt

Note: Nutritional yeast flakes are optional, they add a slight cheesy flavour. But please don't use brewers yeast or bakers yeast, they're completely different.

1 Put all the pesto ingredients into a food processor and whiz them all up until you reach a smooth sauce. Open the lid and push the mixture down into the blades if it sticks to the sides of the bowl.

2 Use just 2 tablespoons of the pesto, or to taste in the salad

Baby Spinach & Fig

Serves 1

FOR THE SALAD

30g baby spinach
1 fig, cut into wedges lengthways
pecan nuts, to garnish

FOR THE DRESSING

1 teaspoon linseed (flax) oil
1 teaspoon rich, thick balsamic vinegar

Toss the baby spinach leaves in the dressing. Arrange the spinach leaves on a small plate, and top with figs and pecan nuts

This is an enjoyable snack, half savoury, half fruit and 100% delicious!

Turkish Shepherd's Salad

Serves 3 - 4

FOR THE SALAD

100g red cabbage, sliced fine on the mandolin
1/3 cucumber, sliced
1 flat leaf lettuce, chopped or torn
2 large carrots, grated
2 red tomatoes, cubed
50g parsley (otherwise dill, but nice with coriander too)
¼ red onion, thinly sliced

FOR THE DRESSING

1 lemon, juiced
2 – 3 tablespoons olive oil
¼ teaspoon Himalayan salt

This is such a common salad in Turkey, but totally tasty. For our honeymoon, we did a yacht tour of the southern Turkish coast, and we had many many variations of this salad. Sometimes the chef would take out an ingredient or two, sometimes add them in, you could also add olives to this recipe.

Green Leaves & Pomegranate

Serves 1 - 2

FOR THE SALAD

150g mixed green leaves
100g pomegranate
¼ red onion, chopped very finely
1 tablespoon linseed (flax) oil
drizzle linseed (flax) oil
drizzle balsamic vinegar
pine nuts, to garnish

" Pomegrates are massively high in antioxidants which are very
good at killing off dental bacteria. In the south of Turkey
you can just walk along the street and pick them
off a tree, but the best ones I've ever had came from Iran. "

Mexican Salad

Serves 1

FOR THE SALAD

1 fresh sweet corn, cut off the cob
10 cherry tomatoes, quartered
1 spring onion, sliced
½ avocado, chopped into cubes
20g coriander (cilantro)

FOR THE DRESSING

2 tablespoons linseed (flax) oil
zested rind of half a lime
½ lime, juiced
½ teaspoon cumin
½ teaspoon finely chopped red chilli

"An easy way to make a salad is to think of all the ingredients
native to a particular country of the world,
then mix them together. That's what I've done here."

Bulls Blood Lettuce & Peach

Serves 1

FOR THE SALAD

50g bulls blood lettuce
½ avocado, sliced
½ peach, sliced
pumpkin seeds, to garnish

FOR THE DRESSING

1 tablespoon olive oil
1 tablespoon lemon juice
pinch Himalayan salt

" NO – I'm not putting Bulls Blood in my salads! It's a leaf
you could use other green leaves in this salad or mixed leaves. "

Italian Noodle Salad

Serves 1

FOR THE SALAD

1 courgette (zucchini), cut into noodles on the mandolin
30g sun dried tomato, soaked in water for a few hours
¼ cup black olives
1/3 cup pine nuts
1 fresh tomato

FOR THE DRESSING

½ lemon, juiced
¼ teaspoon of Italian seasoning
1 – 2 tablespoons olive oil
pinch of cayenne pepper – optional

"A good way to come up with new recipes is just to think of all the vegetables, herbs and spices common to a specific country or region and combine them, that's what I've done here."

Baby Aubergine (Eggplant) Italian Style

Serves 1

FOR THE SALAD

150g baby spinach
6 cherry tomatoes, quartered
1 baby aubergine, marinated
olives, to garnish
pine nuts, to garnish
capers, to garnish

FOR THE AUBERGINE (EGGPLANT) MARINADE

2 tablespoons olive oil
2 tablespoons tamari

FOR THE DRESSING

1 tablespoon olive oil
1 teaspoon rich and sticky balsamic

Marinate the sliced aubergine for 3 hours – it will soak up the flavours of the marinade nicely.

Courgette Noodles in Truffle Cream Sauce

Serves 1

FOR THE SALAD

    1 courgette (zucchini), cut into noodles on the mandolin

FOR THE TRUFFLE CREAM SAUCE

    ½ cup cashews
    ½ cup water
    1 tablespoon truffle infused olive oil
    ½ teaspoon Himalayan salt

For the truffle cream sauce, put all the cream ingredients in the blender and blend until smooth. If it won't turn over in the blender properly, add more water. Or, if it is not smooth enough, blend more.

 One of the simplest, and yet one of my favourite salads. It's like eating tagliatelle in a creamy béchamel sauce.

Kebab Shop Red Cabbage

Serves 3 - 4

FOR THE SALAD

    ½ red cabbage
    1 lemon, juiced
    2 – 3 tablespoons olive oil
    1/3 teaspoon Himalayan salt

Finely slice the red cabbage on the mandolin, the finer the better. Add the Himalayan salt, olive oil and lemon juice. Then let the cabbage sit, the longer the better. If you slice the cabbage fine it will be ready in an hour or two. This salad is really nice even the next day!

Note: The finer you slice the cabbage, the quicker it will wilt and marinate.

When we're out of the house, we try and eat as healthy as possible. Having a Turkish wife, sometimes we end up with a box full of salad from a kebab shop. This recipe is how they prepare their cabbage. The longer it sits, the better it gets. You could even prepare it the night before.

Asparagus & Bell Pepper

Serves 1 - 2

FOR THE SALAD

100g asparagus, sliced fine diagonally
½ red pepper, finely diced
½ yellow pepper, finely diced
3-4 basil leaves, finely sliced
¼ cup black olives
¼ cup green olives
¼ cup pine nuts

FOR THE DRESSING

1 tablespoon olive oil
1 teaspoon of rich, thick balsamic

Note: Tasty ingredients make a tasty salad. I recommend you get really good quality olives for this salad because cheap olives won't be so nice. Go to www.lushsalads.co.uk to get the olives we love!

Morocc

Middle

Indi

Moroccan Orange Salad

FOR THE SALAD

    2 oranges, peeled and sliced thin
    ¼ cup kalamata olives
    1 small red onion, sliced thin
    1 teaspoon olive oil
    ¼ cinnamon
    big pinch Himalayan salt

Other spices you could put in here are ¼ teaspoon paprika
and a ¼ teaspoon cumin. To make this into
more of a dessert, take out the olives
and onion you could put in dates, almonds, and vanilla.

Moroccan Carrot Salad with Spices

Serves 1

FOR THE SALAD

200g Carrot, grated fine
70g raisins, (to soften them, you can soak the raisins in water
for a few hours)
50g pistachios
30g coriander (cilantro), chopped
1 small lemon, juiced
1 small red onion, chopped fine

FOR THE DRESSING

1 tablespoon olive oil
1/3 teaspoon cumin. ground
½ teaspoon ginger, zested
1/3 teaspoon cardamom, ground
¼ teaspoon Himalayan salt
¼ teaspoon paprika

This would be an excellent salad for anyone desiring
a more filling and heavier element in their diet.

Sprouted Quinoa Tabbouleh

Serves 1 - 2

FOR THE SALAD

    350g sprouted quinoa
    100g chopped cucumber, diced small
    135g tomato, diced small
    75g red onion, diced small
    25g parsley
    10g mint leaves

FOR THE DRESSING

    3 tablespoons olive oil
    2 teaspoons lemon juice
    1 teaspoon cumin
    ½ teaspoon cinnamon
    Himalayan salt & freshly ground pepper

TO SPROUT QUINOA

Soak the quinoa in water overnight. Drain the quinoa the next day in a sieve and rinse with water. The quinoa will be ready to use.

" Tabbouleh, also known as Tabouleh or Tabouli, is Syria's national dish. In England we tend to be sold on the idea of using lots of bulgur (which I have substituted with sprouted quinoa), but it can also include very little bulgur or quinoa and it can be mainly a herb salad using lots of parsley and mint. "

Creamy Fattoush

Serves 1 - 2

FOR THE SALAD

250g cherry tomatoes chopped in half
1 cucumber chopped into small pieces
½ cup parsley chopped
½ cup mint, chopped
1 red bell pepper, diced
1 small red onion, diced
10 red radishes, sliced

FOR THE CASHEW SAUCE

1 cup of cashews
1/2 cup of water
1 lemon, juiced
1/8 teaspoon Himalayan salt

In a blender, blend all the cashew sauce ingredients until smooth.
Mix everything together and serve.

Fattoush is a Levantine salad made from several seasonal
garden vegetables and herbs. The vegetables are cut
into relatively larges pieces. Here I have mixed it with
a cashew based alternative to yoghurt to make it creamy.

Okra - Banana Korma

Serves 1

FOR THE SALAD

1 plantain, over ripe, sliced (or just use another banana)
1 banana
60g okra, sliced
1 tablespoon coriander (cilantro), or Methi (herb)

FOR THE COCONUT CREAM SAUCE

100ml coconut cream
1 teaspoon curry powder
¼ teaspoon Himalayan salt
cayenne pepper, big pinch

66 I love Indian food because of the emphasis on vegetables,
and the spices are very good for you. Now we've made it into a
salad that also does away with the heavy use of cooked oils. 99

Raita Salad

Serves 2

FOR THE SALAD

  1 large cucumber, sliced
  1 tablespoon mint, chopped
  ¼ teaspoon garlic, zested
  1 heaped tablespoon finely chopped mint

FOR THE CASHEW SAUCE

  1 cup cashews
  ½ cup water
  1 lemon, juiced
  2 big pinches, Himalayan salt

In a blender, blend all the cashew sauce ingredients until smooth.
Then mix everything together and serve.

This salad is based on Raita, the condiment from India. Other
ingredients you could use are coriander (cilantro), cumin,
cayenne pepper, and onions. Normally, Raita would be
served chilled and has a cooling effect on the palate which
makes a good counter balance to spicy Indian dishes.

Banglatown Salad

Serves 3

FOR THE SALAD

½ white cabbage, sliced fine on the mandolin
1/3 cucumber, sliced into matchsticks on the mandolin
2 or 3 tomatoes, diced
1 bunch coriander, chopped fine
1 green chilli, finely chopped

FOR THE DRESSING

2 – 4 tablespoons lemon juice
2 – 4 tablespoons olive oil
pinch Himalayan salt

TIP FOR CUTTING CABBAGE ON THE MANDOLIN
Cut the cabbage in half through the stem, but don't cut the stem because when slicing the cabbage on the mandolin, the stem holds all the leaves together and makes your work much easier!

> We're always working on the weekends conducting seminars and trainings, so our day off is on a Monday. One Monday we went to London's Brick Lane – which is the heart of the Bangladeshi community in London. I guess you could call this a Bangladeshi take on an European salad.

Indian Cauliflower Salad

Serves 1

FOR THE SALAD

200g cauliflower broken into very small florets
60g red cabbage, shredded
80g carrots cut in matchsticks
chives, snipped to garnish

FOR THE COCONUT CREAM DRESSING

200ml coconut cream
1 tablespoon curry powder
½ teaspoon Himalayan salt
cayenne pepper, big pinch

" Cauliflower can be very nice raw, it's just
about breaking it into small enough florets. "

Thai

Japane

Chin

Carambola & Oyster Mushrooms

Serves 1

FOR THE SALAD

150g oyster mushrooms
70g bean sprouts
½ star fruit, cut into slices

FOR THE THAI MARINADE

2 tablespoons of tamari
1 tablespoon lime juice
1 teaspoon agave syrup
1/8 teaspoon garlic, zested
1/8 teaspoon red chilli, cut really small

Marinade the mushrooms for 10 minutes, they will soak up all the taste and flavour quite quickly.

Yam Pak

Serves 1

FOR THE SALAD

    50g baby aubergine, sliced
    1 star fruit, sliced fine
    30g fine green beans
    1 small red onion, sliced fine on the mandolin

FOR THE THE AUBERGINE MARINADE

    ¼ cup oilve oil
    ¼ cup tamari

FOR THE RED ONION MARINADE

    1 tablespoon olive oil
    1 tablespoon tamari
    1 tablespoon maple syrup

FOR THE DRESSING

    1 tablespoon tamari
    1 tablespoon lime juice
    1 teaspoon agave
    1/8 teaspoon garlic, zested
    1/8 teaspoon red chilli, cut really small

1 Marinate the sliced aubergine for 3 hours – it will soak up the flavours of the marinade nicely.

2 Marinate the sliced red onion for 3 hours – it will soften and mellow the onion.

Pad Thai

Serves 1

FOR THE SALAD

1 courgette (zucchini), with skin peeled, sliced into superfine noodles on the mandolin
90g bean sprouts
½ small carrot, sliced into noodles on the mandolin
zest the rind of one lime
1/2 small red onion, marinated
cashews to garnish

FOR THE RED ONION MARINADE

1 tablespoon Tamari
1 tablespoon olive oil
1 tablespoon maple syrup

FOR THE THAI DRESSING

2 tablespoons tamari
1 tablespoons lime juice
1 teaspoon agave syrup
1/8 teaspoon garlic, zested
1/8 teaspoon red chilli, cut really small
1/8 teaspoon ginger, zested

1. Marinade the red onion for at least 1 hour or more in the marinade.

2. Put the rest of the salad in a bowl and mix with the dressing. Place on a plate and top with the marinated red onion and cashews.

Som Tam

Serves 1

2 green papaya (substitute with green mango if can't find papaya), sliced into thin strips on the mandolin
1 red tomato (optional), diced

2 tablespoons agave
1 tablespoon tamari
2 tablespoons lime juice
¼ teaspoon zested garlic
¼ teaspoon finely chopped red chilli

" In Thailand, lots of sugar would be mixed in with this salad. Here I've used agave syrup instead. Alternatively, you could use sweet ripe Pakistan honey mangoes combined with the green papaya / green mango to add sweetness in a more natural way. "

Thai Kale

Serves 1 - 2

FOR THE SALAD

200g kale
1 red onion, sliced fine
35g carrots, cut into matchsticks
35g bean sprouts

FOR THE RED ONION MARINADE

2 tablespoons olive oil
2 tablespoons tamari
2 tablespoons maple syrup

FOR THE DRESSING

8 tablespoons lime Juice
4 tablespoons agave
4 tablespoons tamari

Marinate the red onion for at least 2 hours (the longer the better).

If you don't have limes, you could use lemon instead, though it won't be quite as authentic.

Thai Crunchy Salad

Serves 1 - 2

FOR THE SALAD

1/2 cucumber, cut into thin strips
1 red pepper, cut into long strips
1 medium carrot, cut into thin strips
70g bean sprouts
1 medium red onion, sliced and marinated
20 mint leaves, cut into thin strips

FOR THE RED ONION MARINADE

2 tablespoons tamari
2 tablespoons olive oil
2 tablespoons maple syrup

FOR THE DRESSING

1 tablespoon tamari
1 tablespoon lime juice
1 tablespoon agave
1 teaspoon lemon grass, sliced fine
1/2 teaspoon red chilli, minced fine

Bean Sprout & Capsicum

Serves 1

FOR THE SALAD

100g bean sprouts
½ red pepper, cut into strips
30g savoy cabbage, finely sliced
10g arame seaweed, soaked for 30 mins in water
¼ teaspoon garlic zest
¼ teaspoon finely chopped red chilli

CHOOSE A DRESSING:

TAHINI LIME DRESSING

2 tablespoons lime juice
1 tablespoon tahini
1 teaspoon tamari
¼ teaspoon ginger zest

ORANGE & MISO DRESSING

3 tablespoons orange juice
1 tablespoon white miso
¼ teaspoon ginger zest

"
This is one of the new recipes I created for the book. In our
taste tests, we just couldn't
work out which dressing we preferred, so we included both.
"

Thai Bean Sprout & Coconut Salad

Serves 1 - 2

FOR THE SALAD

100g bean sprouts
25g brown coconut meat shavings, on the mandolin
½ small red onion
¼ red pepper, chopped fine
¼ cup chopped coriander (cilantro) chopped

FOR THE RED ONION MARINADE

1 tablespoon maple syrup
1 tablespoon olive oil
1 tablespoon tamari

FOR THE THAI DRESSING

2 tablespoons tamari
1 tablespoon lime juice
1 teaspoon agave syrup
1/8 teaspoon garlic, zested
1/8 teaspoon red chilli, cut really small

Marinade the red onion for at least 2 hours. The longer you marinade the onion, the better.

Tropical Delight

Serves 2

FOR THE SALAD

½ cucumber, sliced fine on the mandolin
¼ brown coconut flesh, sliced fine on the mandolin
1 papaya, diced
20 fresh mint leaves

FOR THE DRESSING

3 tablespoons linseed (flax) oil
1 lime, juiced
1 lemon grass, minced fine
½ teaspoon ginger, zested
¼ teaspoon red chilli, zested

To crack open a brown coconut, give it a good whack with a hammer. You could also used desiccated coconut for this recipe, or even fresh jelly from a young green coconut.

Papaya & Sprouted Quinoa

Serves 1

FOR THE SALAD

100g papaya, diced
100g tomato, diced
100g sprouted quinoa
1 tablespoon chives, snipped

FOR THE DRESSING

1 tablespoon linseed (flax) oil
1 teaspoon lemon grass, chopped fine
pinch Himalayan salt
pinch Chinese 5 spice

To give the salad shape, you can press the salad into a rosti ring (steel ring available from kitchen shops) and garnish the salad with diced papaya and tomato.

TO SPROUT THE QUINOA
Soak the quinoa in water overnight. It will start to sprout very quickly, strain the water off the next day, the sprouts will be ready.

> " Using a rosti ring to present salads can create an extra element of excitement to impress your guests. "

Japanese Noodles 1

Serves 1

FOR THE SALAD

100g beetroot, spiralised on the noodle maker
150g butternut squash, spiralised on the noodle maker
80g arame seaweed, soaked in water for at least 15 mins
80g hijiki seaweed, soaked in water for at least 15 mins
2 spring onions (scallion), sliced small

FOR THE DRESSING

2 tablespoons <u>white</u> miso
½ teaspoon ginger, zested
2.5 tablespoon mirin
2.5 tablespoon rice vinegar

"
Sugar in all forms is detrimental to our health and a great way
to get fat! By far the worst form of sugar is grains because grains
are 80% sugar, which is what noodles are normally made out of.
But noodles don't taste of anything – so guess what we're
addicted to? THE SHAPE! The noodle maker tool turns hard and
root vegetables into lovely healthy and low calorie noodles.
"

Japanese Noodles 2

Serves 1

FOR THE SALAD

150g butternut squash (or carrot) noodles, made fine on the noodle maker
150g shitake
20g arame, soaked in water for 30 minutes, water drained
1 spring onion (scallion), sliced

FOR THE MUSHROOM MARINADE

50ml olive oil
50ml tamari

FOR THE DRESSING

1 tablespoon linseed (flax) oil
1 tablespoon mirin
1 tablespoon tamari

Marinate the mushrooms for 30 minutes in the marinade. They will soak up the flavours and the oils just nice!

"
Any time you can add seaweed to your diet, I highly recommend it because we are generally demineralised and seaweeds contain an abundance of all minerals from the sea.
"

Oriental Noodles

Serves 3

FOR THE SALAD

100g desiccated coconut
4 spring onions (scallion), finely chopped
1 butternut squash, cut into fine noodles with a noodle maker
1 red pepper, diced
1 small bunch basil, nicely chopped

FOR THE DRESSING

1 lime rind, zested
1 lime, juiced
¼ teaspoon ginger, zested
2 – 4 tablespoons tamari sauce
2 – 4 tablespoons linseed (flax) oil

" This has to be one of my guests favourite salads. Of course it tastes great, but I think the real secret to it's success is that the squash and desiccated coconut make it a heavy and filling dish – something that people sometimes miss when they start eating healthier. "

Cauliflower Sushi Maki

Serves 3 - 5

2 cups cauliflower florets
10 sheets nori seaweed
1½ cups cashews
1 red bell pepper, cut into long thin strips
1 avocado, cut into long thin strips
1 cucumber, cut into long thin strips
3 spring onions (scallion) cut into long thin strips
pickled ginger to serve
tamari to serve

1 Put the cashews in to a food processor, process them fine until they are a coarse flour consistency. Empty the cashews in to a separate bowl. Repeat with cauliflower. Mix the cauliflower and cashews together with your hands. The mixture should take shape well when you squeeze it together.

2 Lay the nori sheet flat. Spread the cashew-cauliflower mixture thinly and evenly onto the nori sheet, leaving 1 inch margins at both the top and the bottom of the nori sheet.

3 Place the finely sliced avocado, cucumber, spring onions (scallion) along the bottom of edge of the cashew-cauliflower mixture on the nori sheet.

4 Starting at the bottom, roll the nori sheet with toppings up tightly. To make the roll stick, wet the last 1cm flap of nori before you roll it. Then cut into segments.

5 Serve the sushi with pickled ginger and tamari.

> " Cauliflower and vegetable sushi becomes really light and healthy. The pickled ginger and tamari give it the taste. "

Green Courgette Noodle with Bok Choy & Shiitake

Serves 1 - 2

FOR THE SALAD

2 courgettes, cut into superfine noodles on the mandolin (smallest setting)
2 baby bok choy, sliced fine (or use mature bok choy)
200g shiitake mushrooms, marinated for ½ hour
2 spring onion (scallion), sliced fine

FOR THE MARINADE

½ cup tamari
½ cup olive oil

FOR THE DRESSING

4 tablespoons mirin
2 tablespoons rice wine vinegar
½ teaspoon paprika

Marinate the shiitake mushrooms in the tamari and olive oil for 30 minutes

Japanese Cucumber

Serves 2 – 3 as a side salad

FOR THE SALAD

1 cucumber, sliced on a mandolin
1 small garlic clove, zested
½ teaspoon ginger, zested

FOR THE DRESSING

2 tablespoons tamari
1 teaspoon mirin
1 teaspoon rice vinegar

TO GARNISH

½ spring onion (scallion), finely sliced
½ red pepper, diced
½ teaspoon sesame seeds, sprinkle

"
This is more of a side salad to be served with other Japanese
food. You could serve this with the other Japanese
recipes in this book: sushi maki, Japanese
seaweed and Japanese noodles. Of course you
would have to round your evening off with some Karaoke!
"

Japanese Bean & Pea

Serves 1

FOR THE SALAD

160g mange tout, cut into diamonds
180g fresh baby peas
20g coriander (cilantro) finely chopped
2 tablespoons dried seaweed flakes

FOR THE JAPANESE DRESSING

3 tablespoons mirin
3 tablespoons rice vinegar
1½ tablespoons white miso (no other colour miso please! Only white!)

The dried seaweed flakes, if you're having trouble getting them, go to our website www.lushsalads.co.uk and look for the seaweed salad.

Maitake Mushroom Salad

Serves 1

FOR THE SALAD

75g maitake mushrooms
20g red chard (or other soft leaf)
20g mizuna (or rocket)
10g basil
1 small red onion, sliced
pine nuts to garnish

FOR THE RED ONION MARINADE

1 tablespoon maple syrup
1 tablespoon tamari sauce
1 tablespoon olive oil

FOR THE MUSHROOM MARINADE

2 tablespoons olive oil
1 teaspoon rich, thick balsamic

FOR THE GREEN LEAF DRESSING

1 teaspoon olive oil
1 teaspoon lemon juice
pinch Himalayan salt
pinch black pepper

1 Marinate the red onion first for at least 1 hour. Although the onion only gets better the longer you marinate it. You could marinate it a day in advance.

2   Marinate the maitake mushrooms in the olive oil and thick balsamic for 30 minutes. They don't need too long because they will soak up the flavours quickly.

3 Toss the leaves in leaf dressing. Arrange leaves on a bowl or plate, top with maitake mushrooms and red onions. Sprinkle with pine nuts.

Japanese Seaweed Salad

Serves 1 as a side salad

FOR THE SALAD

10g dried wakame, soaked in water for 20 minutes
5g arame or hijiki soaked in water for 20 minutes
red bell pepper, finely chopped.
spring onion (scallion), finely chopped.

FOR THE JAPANESE DRESSING

2 tablespoons rice vinegar
2 tablespoons mirin
1 tablespoon <u>white</u> miso

Drain the seaweed of water, pour the dressing on top, and decorate with the red bell pepper and spring onion.

" People ask me what I eat when I eat out. Whilst I'm not fanatical about any of this, I tend not to eat grains or silly things and normally just opt for a Japanese seaweed salad. "

Medicinal Mushroom Salad

Serves 2

FOR THE SALAD

100g shiitake mushroom
100g maitake mushroom
70g walnuts
50g rocket

FOR THE DRESSING

2 tablespoons olive oil
1 tablespoon honey
1 teaspoon sherry vinegar
pinch Himalayan salt

First mix up the dressing and pour it on the mushrooms, they will soak up the flavour, then get going with the rest of the salad.

" Ordinary shop bought mushrooms contain a lot of mycotoxins, so rather than be beaten, I've switched to using medicinal mushrooms. Both shiitake and maitake mushrooms are therapeutic for almost every system of the body and can be bought from a good supermarket. "

Bok Choy

Serves 2

3 heads of bok choy, sliced
1 small red onion, chopped into fine cubes
½ red bell pepper, chopped into fine cubes
1 small carrot, chopped into fine cubes
1 tablespoon sesame seeds to garnish

3 tablespoons linseed (Flax Seed Oil)
3 tablespoons tamari
¾ teaspoon zested ginger
¾ teaspoon finely minced red chilli
¾ teaspoon zested garlic

Mix half the dressing with the bok choy and thoroughly coat. Mix the remainder of the dressing with the carrots, bell pepper and onion and thoroughly coat. Arrange the bok choy on plates, top with the diced vegetable mix. Garnish with sesame seeds.

Bok Choy & Cauliflower

Serves 1

FOR THE SALAD

200g cauliflower, broken into small florets
100g baby bok choy broken into leaves (or mature bok choy sliced)
sesame seeds to garnish

FOR THE CHINESE DRESSING

4 tablespoons tamari
2 tablespoons tahini
2 tablespoons runny honey
1 tablespoon ginger, zested
chilli flakes, big pinch

Chinese Fortune Cookie Quote:

" If you get flowers in your Bok Choy it's your lucky day! "

Chinese Pear & Bean Sprout

Serves 1

FOR THE SALAD

70g bean sprouts
50g sugar snaps, cut into diamonds
65g celery, sliced
25g coriander (cilantro)
2 conference pears, sliced into thin strips on the mandolin
sesame seeds to decorate

FOR THE CHINESE DRESSING

4 tablespoons tamari
2 tablespoons tahini
2 tablespoons honey (runny) or agave syrup
1 tablespoon ginger, zested
chilli flakes, big pinch

" YUM! "

Vegetable Chop Suey

Serves 2

FOR THE SALAD

300g bean sprouts
100g mange tout, cut into diamond shapes
2 medium carrots, grated
1 red bell pepper, sliced into thin strips
3 spring onions (scallion), sliced
1 courgette (zucchini), cut the courgette in half lengthways, then slice into thin half moon shapes on the mandolin

FOR THE DRESSING

¼ cup extra virgin olive oil
¼ cup white miso
3 tablespoons brown rice vinegar
3 tablespoons umeboshi plum paste
1 tablespoon ginger, zested

" As a child, every now and then my father would order a
Chinese take-away,
this recipe really reminds me of the chop suey we would get. "

Chinese Leaves with Ginger Dressing

Serves 1 - 2

FOR THE SALAD

- ½ chinese leaf lettuce
- 20g coriander (cilantro)
- 40g mooli (daikon) or red radishes cut in matchsticks
- 100g sugar snaps sliced
- 1 spring onion, spiced
- 1 tablespoon sesame seeds

FOR THE DRESSING

- 2 tablespoons mirin
- 2 tablespoons linseed oil
- 2 tablespoons tamari
- 2 tablespoons rice vinegar
- ½ teaspoon of ginger, zested

Fruit

I like it sweet

and Juicy!

Sweet Syrup Dressings

Syrups are the dressings of the dessert world.

To make delicious flavoured syrups, start with agave syrup, which tastes fairly neutral. Then you can infuse flavours into the agave syrup just by putting the whole ingredients in and letting them sit. Here's some ideas:

Vanilla Syrup

250ml bottle of Agave, put 1 or 2 whole vanilla pods in there. This will keep almost forever. Just keep topping up the bottle of agave with fresh agave each time you use it. Bottles I've done like this last about 1 year before the vanilla pod starts losing it's fragrance and I have to use a new vanilla pod.

Cinnamon Syrup

Same as above, but with a cinnamon quill.

Ginger & Lemongrass

¼ cup agave syrup
3cm of lemongrass, sliced fine
3cm of ginger, sliced fine

Put the finely sliced lemongrass and ginger into the cup with the agave. Mix well, and let it sit for 1 hour or more. After an hour the flavours will be well infused into the agave syrup, discard the lemongrass and ginger and pour onto the dessert.

Mint Syrup

Chop up a bunch of fresh mint, pack it tight into a glass jar and fill the jar up all the way with agave syrup. Make sure you get rid of all the air bubbles amongst the chopped mint. Leave the jar of agave and mint in the fridge overnight. You will have a lovely minty syrup! Note: fresh mint will go off. This syrup will only be good for a day. Pull the mint leaves out.
You could also try with dried mint or essential oil.

Design Your Own Syrup

Making your own syrups are both fun and easy. Try different infusions of spices, herbs or flowers.

Decadent Berries
& Balsamic

Serves 1

FOR THE SALAD

   blueberries
   raspberries
   blackberries
   strawberries
   grapes
   balsamic, rich and thick

Cover the berries in a good dowsing of high end, rich and sticky balsamic.

Note: Cheap balsamic will not do! Because cheap balsamic is not aged properly and it is mixed with a lot of red wine vinegar which will make this recipe taste awful! If you don't have a top quality balsamic, go to our website www.lushsalads.co.uk for a bottle of this magical stuff.

 It's surprising how decadent simple berries can taste with a really good balsamic. In Italy it is normal to put balsamic on strawberries. Try it, I think you'll like it!

Apple Cake Salad

Serves 1

FOR THE SALAD

    2 crisp and sweet apples, grated
    2 tablespoons coconut cream
    2 tablespoons maple syrup
    40g pecan nuts
    pinch cinnamon

TO DECORATE

    coconut cream
    pecans

SERVING IDEA
Place a rosti ring* on the plate, softly press the mixture down in the ring with a spoon and when you are done, remove it slowly. Decorate with coconut cream and pecans or however you like!

*Rosti rings are simple stainless steel rings used to press food in. They can be bought from catering shops, but you can also use an empty round cardboard container and cut the ends off.

Grated apple never tasted so good! When we're stuffed full of savoury food and can't possibly eat any more, we always make room for this apple cake salad.

Cocktail Fruits with Passion Crème

Serves 2

2 bananas
400g strawberries
8 kiwi fruits
1 orange or grapefruit
1 pack of cocktail sticks

FOR THE PASSION CRÈME

1 cup cashews
½ cup orange juice
1 lime, juiced
¼ cup agave syrup

1   Cut a slice off the bottom of the orange so that it will stand up.

2   Cut up the fruit into bite size chunks and skewer onto cocktail sticks. Spike the fruit skewers into the orange like a pincushion.

3   Put all the passion crème ingredients into a blender and blend until smooth. If you don't have a high end or commercial blender, first soak the cashews in water for a few hours, this will be much easier for you blender. If the crème is not turning over properly in the blender, add some more orange juice.

" On New Years Eve, my mother would make several different oranges or grapefruits and stick an assortment of nibbles on the cocktail sticks. At my parties it never fails to impress my guests. "

Melon Balls in Lime Syrup

Serves 1

FOR THE SALAD

watermelon balls
canteloupe melon balls
galia melon balls
honeydew melon balls
mint leaves to decorate

FOR THE SYRUP

1 teaspoon agave syrup
1 teaspoon lime juice

Make the melon balls using a melon baler, which is a small and cheap kitchen tool. Adjust the lime and agave to taste.

 Making and presenting melons in balls takes a little time, and it also impresses your guests. Presentation is important.

Fresh Filling Passion

Serves 1 - 2

FOR THE SALAD

    Coconut jelly from 1 young green coconut
    1 banana, cut into slices
    2 passion fruit, halved and scooped out
    10 rose petals, cut into fine strips

Young green coconuts are so fresh and juicy compared to the old brown coconuts. The coconut meat is actually more like the consistency of lasagne. Young green coconuts can be bought from your local Afro-Caribbean and Thai shops. You can also get them from us at www.lushsalads.co.uk

"
My normal diet is quite boring and basic. One morning my wife declared she'd had enough wheatgrass juice and said I would have to prove my love for her by making something fresh, filling and nice! This salad did the trick!
"

Grapefruit & Cashews

Serves 1

FOR THE SALAD

1 pink grapefruit, in segments
2 basil leaves, sliced fine
¼ teaspoon red chillies, finely chopped
1 teaspoon of Thai dressing
1 teaspoon of cashews, finely chopped

FOR THE THAI DRESSING

2 tablespoons tamari
1 tablespoon lime juice
1 teaspoon agave syrup
1/8 teaspoon garlic, zested
1/8 teaspoon red chilli, cut really small

The idea here is from south east Asian cuisine. The combination
seems strange at first, but this is so light and
refreshing, and the spiciness adds a wicked twist to it.

Exotic Fruit Baskets

melon(s) to cut into baskets
lychees
raspberries
blackberries
pomegranate
mango
kiwi
grape

Presentation can make such a huge difference. I spent a
little time carving out the baskets from the melons,
but when my wife saw them,
she was so happy it perked her up for the rest of the day!

Lychees in Ginger & Lemongrass Syrup

Serves 1

FOR THE SALAD

12 lychees
1 star fruit, cut into slices
lime rind to garnish

FOR THE SYRUP

¼ cup agave syrup
3cm of lemongrass, sliced fine
3cm of ginger, sliced fine

Put the finely sliced lemongrass and ginger into the cup with the agave. Mix well, and let it sit for 1 hour or more. After an hour the flavours will be well infused into the agave syrup, discard the lemongrass and ginger and pour onto the dessert.

Dry Fruit Dessert

Serves 1 - 2

FOR THE SALAD

7 prunes, soaked in water for 4 hours or more
7 non-sulphured dried apricots, soaked in water for 4 hours or more
1 banana, sliced
small carton coconut cream

Drizzle with coconut cream - And you're good to go!!

Coconut cream is the cream version of coconut milk. It is not creamed coconut which comes as a hard block.

" We would have a variation of this for breakfast as children, also served as desserts, it is a filling meal for the winter. "

Sweet Fruit & Chocolate

Serves 1 - 2

FOR THE SALAD

    8 medjool dates, pitted
    2 ripe figs, in segments
    pecans, to garnish

FOR THE CHOCOLATE SAUCE

    ½ cup maple syrup
    ½ cup raw African cacao powder
    ¼ cup Philippines coconut oil

1 Coconut oil is solid in colder climates, and is an oil in hotter climates. If the coconut oil is not runny, first put the whole coconut oil tub in a bowl of hot water for 30 minutes. This will melt the oil and make it runny.

2 In a blender, pour in the maple syrup and coconut oil first, and cacao powder last. Blend until smooth.

Coconut Oil Note
There is a wide range of quality with coconut oil. I use Philippines coconut oil because it has a beautiful aroma. This makes a big difference in how the chocolate sauce turns out.

Cacao Note
Out of all the raw chocolate powders we have found African to be the tastiest. You can get it from us at www.LushSalads.co.uk otherwise use Green and Black's organic coco powder.

" Most of the people in our company are women, so these sweet fruits with a chocolate sauce is always a winner! Other fruits that go well with chocolate are; banana, strawberries, and mango. "

Design Your Own Salads & Dressings

Design Your Own Salad

Designing your own salad can be very easy. Here I've broken down the component parts of a salad into pick and mix lists so you can have a go at designing your own tasty salads and dressings.

INSTRUCTIONS
Pick either one, or multiple items from each category below

Base Ingredients
Green leaves, courgette noodles, squash noodles, sprouts such as sunflower or alfalfa, peas, beans

Fatty Things
Olives, avocado, nuts, seeds

Sweet Things
Tomatoes, red, yellow or orange bell peppers, sun dried tomatoes, berries, fruit, root vegetables such as carrots and beetroots

Optional, Salty Things
Olives, seaweed, celery

Optional Fragrant Things
Herbs, spices, ginger, garlic, chilli, edible flowers

Design Your Own Dressing

Tart Liquids
Lemon juice, lime juice, grapefruit juice, orange juice
Vinegars: red wine, rice, white wine, apple cider vinegar, balsamic

Oils
Linseed oil (flax seed oil), olive oil, almond oil, hemp oil, walnut oil

Sweet Things, Optional
Fruit / berry juice, balsamic, white miso

Fragrant Things, Optional
Herbs, garlic, ginger, spices, chillies, citrus zest, tamari

Lush Salads: The Sequel

Register now for Lush Salads: The Sequel and receive express notice of launch dates and other info. Register at:

www.lushsalads.co.uk/thesequel

There is no obligation to buy, so register now and we'll keep you updated!

Get a FREE BOOK

Have you got a salad, dressing or dip that sends your friends and family totally doolally with excitement?

If so, send us your recipe. If it gets into Lush Salads: The Sequel, we will send you the book for free, and publish your name in the book so you can be a co-author! (unless you want to appear as "anonymous" that is).

To share a recipe with us, go to: www.lushsalads.co.uk/share

Note: ONLY 100% vegan, 99% raw and 3000% delicious recipes will be considered. The recipe must be of your own design and not copied or borrowed from a recipe book.

INDEX

You're invited to our

Health & Performance Breakthrough Seminar

We run regular seminars on how you can reach peak levels of health and performance. For up to date seminar details, go to: www.lushsalads.co.uk/breakthrough

On the seminar you will learn:

- How to create massive amounts of personal energy
- How to boost your brain power, mental clarity and focus
- How to lose unwanted weight, the fun way
- How to increase your calmness
- The keys to beautiful skin
- How to solve health problems
- How to protect yourself from osteoporosis
- How to eliminate colds and flu's forever
- How to eliminate headaches forever
- How to eliminate the biggest source of toxins
- You will also learn how the foods you have eaten in the past continue to hinder you now, and what to do about it!

For more dates and details, go to
www.lushsalads.co.uk/breakthrough

Book Request Form

 Phone Requests: 020 7624 4531
International orders phone + 44 207 624 4531
Have your credit card ready

 Internet Requests. Go to www.lushsalads.co.uk

 Postal Requests: Raw Food Party, Flat 1,
140 Goldhurst Terrace, London, NW6 3HP

Yes! Please rush me….…...copies of Lush Salads book at £19.99 each.
Free Shipping for UK orders only. International orders, please phone.

☐ Please subscribe me to Peter's Health & Healing email newsletter
(or go to www.lushsalads.co.uk to subscribe)

BLOCK CAPITALS PLEASE

Name:………………………………………………………………………………………..……………………….

Address:………………………………………………………………………………….……..………….……….

…………………………………………………………………………………………………….……………………

City / Town:……………………………………………………………………………….………………………..

Post Code:……………………………………………………………………………………………..…………...

Telephone:……………………………………………………………………………………………..……………

Email Address:………………………………………………………………………………………..…………...

Cheque Enclosed ☐   Card Details: Visa ☐   Mastercard ☐   Maestro/Switch ☐

……..…………...

Expiry Date:………………………..…...................Valid From Date:………………..……………..

Last 3 Digits on back of card:……………...…..Issue number (Maestro's only)…………..…………..